SICKLE CELL DISEASE

SICKLE CELL DISEASE

JACQUELINE L. HARRIS

Twenty-First Century Medical Library
Twenty-First Century Books
Brookfield, Connecticut

SICKLE CELL DISEASE

Photographs courtesy of John Woike/The Hartford Courant: pp. 14, 45; Photo Researchers, Inc.: pp. 18 (© Ken Eward), 21 (© Bill Longcore), 31 (© Dr. Tony Brain/SPL), 73 (© Simon Fraser/Department of Haematology, RVI, Newcastle/SPL), 74 (© A. Leonara); Visuals Unlimited: p. 22 (Science/© Feininger-Crown-Time-Bloom-Fawcett); © St. Francis Hospital and Medical Center: p. 35; National Institutes of Health: p. 57; Moorland-Spingarn Research Center: p. 60; AP/Wide World Photos: p. 77; SABA: p. 85 (© Ann States)

Published by Twenty-First Century Books
A Division of The Millbrook Press, Inc.
2 Old New Milford Road, Brookfield, Connecticut 06804
www.millbrookpress.com

Library of Congress Cataloging-in-Publication Data
Harris, Jacqueline L.
Sickle cell disease / by Jacqueline Harris.
p. cm. — (Twenty-first century medical library)
Includes bibliographical references and index.
ISBN 0-7613-1459-8 (lib. bdg.)
1. Sickle cell anemia—Juvenile literature. [1. Sickle cell anemia.
2. Diseases.] I. Title. II. Series
RC641.7.S5 H37 2001
616.1'527—dc21   00-047932

CONTENTS

Chapter One

A STATE OF REPEATED PAIN

SAMANTHA

Six-year-old Samantha (not her real name) is a four-foot-tall, thin, pigtailed young lady. Her favorite foods are chicken, pancakes, waffles, orange juice, and most kinds of fruit. She likes to pedal her toy jeep, pretending she's going to the market. Curious and determined, Samantha keeps trying until she's finished a task. Her latest achievements are riding her bike without the training wheels, learning to roller skate, and figuring out how to braid her own hair. She's going into first grade. Samantha is enjoying her life. "I'm so happy I'm born," she says.

Ms. V., her mother, feels good when she hears her daughter sing and laugh because she knows she's well. Ms. V. walks a tightrope of worry every day, watching her child for signs of pain and illness.

You would never know it to look at Samantha but in her short life she has been in the hospital seven times, enduring pain, needles, transfusions, and surgery.

Samantha was born prematurely—a preemie—and weighed just one pound eight ounces at birth.

"I worried about whether she'd survive," says Ms. V. "She was so tiny. Then they told me she had sickle cell disease. It all hit me at once. I was going crazy with worry. I didn't know anything about this disease, didn't know anyone who had it, never thought about it."

"What's sickle cell disease?" asked Ms. V.

"Somebody will talk to you," said the nurse.

A doctor came and explained how sickle-shaped red blood cells block the flow of blood and cause pain and other problems. "The doctor explained that they have medications and things they can do to help her," said Ms. V. But she still worried.

Samantha did well, coming home to her family on Christmas Eve, a little more than two months after she was born. Ms. V. was given a list of instructions—give her penicillin, folic acid, lots of liquids, and don't let her get too warm or too cold. She was told the warning signs to watch for. In particular, Ms. V. was told that if her child's temperature rose to 101, the doctor should be called at once.

Samantha's problems with SCD began when she was about a year old. Her temperature rose to 101, and she was hospitalized. Once in the hospital, one of Samantha's hands began to swell and hurt. She was given medicine for pain and intravenous fluids. After a few days when the fever, pain, and swelling had stopped, Samantha was allowed to go home. Through her fourth year, she was put in the hospital with similar problems six times. Sometimes her feet would swell, sometimes both her hands and feet would swell. Sometimes she needed blood transfusions.

One winter day when she was about five and a half, Samantha developed severe pain in her stomach during kindergarten class. She screamed with pain, calling for her mother. Ms. V., who carries a beeper, was notified at once. "I rushed her in a car to the hospital. She was screaming and she couldn't stand up," says Ms. V.

In the emergency room the doctors discovered that Samantha had appendicitis. She was given a blood transfusion and taken directly to surgery, where her appendix was removed. Right after surgery, Samantha was discovered to have double pneumonia—a serious congestion of the lungs. She was put on a machine called a respirator to help her breathe and transferred to Children's Hospital. After about ten days of treatment with intravenous fluids, pain medicine, and antibiotics, Samantha recovered and was allowed to go home.

"That problem at age five and her birth have been the scariest part of my life with her," says Ms. V. "Now she's running around giving me trouble." But Ms. V. keeps a watchful eye for more problems.

Samantha and her mother have a routine for preventing problems. After brushing her teeth, Samantha has her breakfast and takes her penicillin and folic acid. Then she showers and gets ready for school. Samantha's teacher has a pamphlet that describes warning signs to watch for. The teacher knows Samantha must have lots of fluids and bathroom breaks. The teacher knows how to reach Ms. V. After school there's a snack, nap, homework, and play. Then dinner and more penicillin, a little TV, time with a book, and bed.

Samantha knows to drink lots of fluids and gets her own juice or water. Ms. V. checks Samantha's spleen twice a day, in the morning and the evening. This organ, located just under the ribs on the left, can get swollen with sickled cells and cause lots of problems. "If the spleen sinks in and it's firm, that's good. But if it's hard, that's not good and I take her right in to the doctor," says Ms. V.

"I take her temperature every other day or more often if she's not feeling well," says Ms. V. She checks the whites of Samantha's eyes to see if they're yellow, a sign that could mean gallbladder disease or other problems.

Samantha is starting to ask questions about her disease. "She asks why I feel her stomach. I tell her I need to know if I should take her to the doctor," says Ms. V.

Samantha asks about her penicillin. "If I don't take my medicine will I die?" she says. Her mother tells her that if she skips it three times, it would be a problem. Now, every day, Samantha gets the liquid penicillin bottle when it's time to take it. Her mother is showing her how to measure out a dose.

Samantha loves her doctors and tells them everything that has happened to her as soon as she arrives in the office. "She is really strong—for a little girl to have to go through all she has, she's really strong," says her mother. "She's determined to fight this."

For her part Ms. V. has great hopes for the future health of her child. "Having the doctors there is so helpful. I can call any time and they'll answer my questions." Ms. V. has also met other families who have children with SCD. "We can talk about it. It makes it easier," she says.

VALENCIA

Valencia is just days shy of her twelfth birthday, about to go into the seventh grade. She's small for her age and has lost her left hand and lower right leg to SCD. Valencia has an artificial lower leg and hand. The loss of a hand or foot is a rare complication of SCD. But

Valencia's dark eyes shine with her view of her life. "I'm like a normal person. I do the same things other kids do. I have no limitations. There is nothing special about me," she says.

Valencia takes tap dancing and karate. Her favorite activity is double Dutch rope jumping and she loves to watch wrestling on TV with her brothers and then practice some of the wrestling holds. She likes to watch basketball and enjoys listening to singer Mya belt out "Movin' On."

One of her hobbies is cooking. She makes macaroni and cheese and pizza with pepperoni and "the works." She likes to go places, "just get out of the house and go to the park or the movies." Her next outing is to the store to shop for school. Jeans, sneakers, skirts, and shoes are on her shopping list.

But nothing makes Valencia happier than having a birthday. She already knows what she's getting for this birthday—a poodle. She even has the name picked out; Sassie will be her new canine buddy.

Valencia feels that her greatest achievement was graduating from sixth grade, and she is looking forward to the seventh grade. She gets A's and B's and hopes to be a lawyer someday. "I'm going to help people get the attention they need. Settle cases. If somebody does something bad to somebody else, I'm going to get justice."

Valencia was two and a half years old when she suffered a major sickle cell crisis. She hurt all over and had a high temperature and blood infection (blood poisoning), and finally went into a coma. In the hospital doctors did everything to help her. Four days later her condition improved, but the lack of blood circulation to her left hand and lower leg had destroyed the flesh and surgeons had to amputate them. "There was nothing they could do to save them. They weren't any good," says Valencia. "But I can do stuff."

Valencia Dixson practices her
front kicks in karate class.

Since then, aside from the aches and pains taken care of at home, Valencia has had about three sickling crises that required hospitalization. The last one was just a few weeks ago. Her temperature soared, and the doctors had to struggle to get it down. She hurt all over, and she was given oxygen and painkillers. After four days, she went home.

Valencia does her best to take care of herself. She takes her penicillin and folic acid and drinks lots of liquids. She tires quickly and takes a rest whenever she needs it. She remembers to bundle up before going out in cold weather in double and triple layers and insulated steel-toed boots. "I can't play in the snow. It would numb me up and I'd have to go to the hospital." And she makes sure to eat nourishing food, which she needs because her body burns energy so fast. She enjoys vegetables like collard greens, green beans, corn, black-eyed peas, and fruits like pineapple and watermelon.

Valencia is grateful that she has an artificial leg so she can walk. "Lots of people have to get about in a wheelchair," she says. She is also grateful that her arm wasn't amputated "up higher" than the wrist.

What Valencia wants most in the world is to help people. "I want to be there for them," she says. "My mom was hit by a car and broke her arm. She hurt her leg too and didn't think she'd ever walk again. I talked to her, got her mind off it. I told her that her arm would get better and she would walk. She's walking now.

"I try to be nice and listen to people and be there for them. That's the best thing about me and people like me," Valencia says.

MICHAEL

Nineteen-year-old Michael (not his real name) came to the United States from Ghana to attend college in New England. He had few problems with SCD in Ghana, but the cold winter weather in New England aggravated his disease. He suffered many pain crises, which were treated in the college infirmary. During one crisis he developed a severe blood infection and was taken to the hospital. During two other hospital stays doctors gave him exchange transfusions, replacing all his sickle blood cells with normal blood cells.

About a year later, he suffered severe pain in his hips and legs after riding his bicycle in cold weather. Some months after that his back began to hurt. The pain spread to his hips and thighs, and he began having trouble breathing. In the hospital his condition grew worse. Severe congestion that spread from one lung to the other made it even harder for him to breathe. His back pain became worse. He was given oxygen, antibiotics, strong medicine for pain, and finally an exchange transfusion. His heart struggled to deal with the increased demand to pump blood. Michael died.

An autopsy showed that the end of his left femur—the bone in the thigh that helps form the hip joint—was nearly destroyed by sickle cells. Fatty dead marrow from the destroyed bone had traveled by way of the bloodstream to the blood vessels of the lungs. Many of his lung blood vessels became clogged with debris from the femur and sickled red blood cells, interrupting the lung blood supply, and sabotaging its function as the body's oxygen supplier.

Chapter Two

BETRAYED BY A BLOOD CELL

Abututuo . . . Chwecheechwe . . . Nuidudui . . . Nwiiwii. If you say these words out loud, they sound like words someone in severe pain might use. These are names that different African tribes have given to a sickness that causes a bone-chewing kind of excruciating pain. The names describe what the illness feels like. But the name that scientists and physicians use—sickle cell disease—describes the source of the problem.

We have billions and billions of microscopic red blood cells in our bodies. Looking at them through a microscope, you will see tiny discs, sort of like donuts. These red blood cells are filled with hemoglobin, which gives blood its red color. Traveling around the body through veins and arteries, the red blood cells deliver oxygen breathed in through the lungs to all parts of the body that use oxygen to make energy. The red blood

17

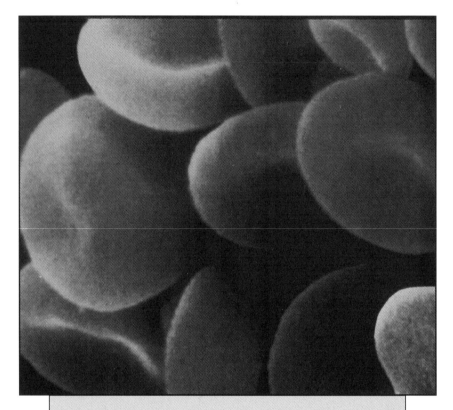

Normal red blood cells

cells' oxygen carriers are the many molecules of hemoglobin inside each cell. Hemoglobin is a chemical made up of iron and protein, which combines with oxygen in the lungs. As the red blood cell carries the hemoglobin through the body, it gradually releases the oxygen.

We inherit the ability to make hemoglobin. Inheritance is carried by chemical structures within the genes in the nucleus of the body's cells. Genes carry the chemical code that is the blueprint for every structure and chemical our body makes—like bones, eyes, skin, and blood. Chemicals called amino acids, which we get from food, link up following the gene's blueprint to form the body's tissues and proteins. People have about 100,000 genes. They are located like beads on a string on 23 pairs of tiny structures within our cells called chromosomes. Genes for each characteristic, like eye color, hair texture, height, and hemoglobin, come in pairs. One of the pair we get from our mother, the other from our father. Depending on how the two genes interact, you may have blue eyes or brown eyes, fine hair or thick hair.

Genes can sometimes change or mutate for reasons we don't understand. Mutated genes are passed on from parent to child through the generations. A mutated gene can cause all kinds of problems if its job is to direct the manufacture of something very important to the body, like that busy oxygen-mover, hemoglobin.

Such a mutation is the problem for people who have sickle cell disease (SCD). Two pairs of normal genes direct the manufacture of the two parts of the normal hemoglobin molecule (HbA). People with SCD have inherited a mutated hemoglobin gene from each parent that carries faulty instructions for making half of the hemoglobin molecule. As a result, their bodies make sickle hemoglobin (HbS). This HbS differs from HbA in that of all the 574 amino acids it is made of, just one is different. The mutation of the gene caused its chemical code to be changed very slightly. The altered code will direct the manufacture of HbS.

THE SICKLING CRISIS

Like HbA, HbS can carry oxygen and is red. But when it releases its oxygen, the problems can begin. The HbS turns from a liquid into a crystal. The HbS crystals join together into many small cords, which then form chains that look like wires twisted together. You can imagine what this crystallization does to the shape of the red blood cell. Cells containing HbA, which stays liquid, are flexible and squeeze into bulletlike shapes as they move through small blood vessels. But red blood cells filled with wirelike crystals of HbS are not flexible. As the cell membrane stretches to contain the strands of HbS crystals, the cells form spikes and sickle shapes. These sickled cells do not move easily through the blood vessels. Sometimes they stick to each other and to the sides of a blood vessel, eventually piling up to form a road block within the blood vessel. This is bad news for the part of the body beyond the blocked blood vessel, because it loses its delivery of oxygen, food, infection fighters, protein, and fluid. Lack of oxygen causes the affected part of the body to produce chemicals that cause pain.

Oxygen will reverse the sickling process, causing the HbS to change from a crystal back to a liquid. But if the blockage remains for very long, tissues deprived of supplies will be damaged. The blockage and the pain can happen anywhere in the body, sometimes in several areas at once. The cell membrane of the red blood cell is damaged by the sickling; after a few sicklings or a prolonged one, the cell may become permanently sickled.

The person with SCD may suffer frequent uncomfortable aches and pains of sickling blockage, which they take care of with heating pads, fluids, rest, and ordinary painkillers. But severe pain, fever, and swelling signal a sickling crisis—time to go to the hospital for strong painkillers and other treatment. It is believed that infection, dehydration, cold weather, overexertion,

Sickled red blood cells

or emotions like anger or fear set the stage for a sick-ling crisis. For most people with SCD, sickling crises are few and far between. But about 15 percent of people with SCD will have three or more major pain crises a year. Each time, tissue and organs can be damaged. The greater the number of crises per year, the greater the chance of dying young.

BONE PAIN:
"A CHEWING PAIN"

One common problem for those with SCD is bone pain. Bones are living tissue that need a blood supply. But

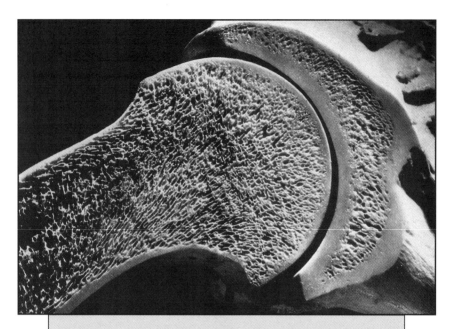

This cross section of a shoulder shows the bone sinusoids that can become blocked by sickled red blood cells.

bones do not have veins and arteries for transporting blood. Instead blood moves through tiny spaces in spongy areas of the bone called sinusoids. Sickled cells can get trapped in these rigid small areas, causing bones and joints to ache. Bone pain can be severe and can last for several days.

Infants with SCD suffer bone pain in their hands and feet—hand/foot syndrome. Loss of blood flow in the hands and feet causes swelling, pain, and fever that can last for about a week. If the baby was not tested at birth, hand/foot syndrome is often the first sign to parents and doctor that the child has been born with SCD.

CHEST SYNDROME:
TROUBLE IN THE OXYGEN TERMINAL

A second serious problem for SCD patients is acute chest syndrome, which affects the lungs. Blood flowing through the lungs picks up oxygen breathed in with air and carries it to all parts of the body. Chest syndrome occurs when small blood vessels are blocked at many points by sickle cell blockages, which, because they reduce oxygen transport, bring on more sickling blockages. Lung infection is another element in this vicious circle, bringing on more sickling, which in turn deprives tissue of infection fighters. As the blood vessels in the lungs become more and more blocked, there is less oxygen available to the body, causing sickling crises in other parts of the body. And if the patient is undergoing a sickling crisis in another part of the body, dead tissue and fat globules can travel by way of the blood to the lungs and cause more blockages. This kind of blockage is called an embolism.

A patient suffering chest syndrome has severe chest pain, cough, fever, and trouble breathing. Bone pain in the ribs will make each breath painful. Acute chest syndrome can be fatal. Even if the patient recovers, the syndrome can recur, each time causing more damage to the delicate lung tissue. Chronic lung disease can damage the heart, which must work much harder to move blood through the lungs.

PAIN IN THE ABDOMEN

Two major organs within the abdomen can be damaged by sickling blockages: the liver and the spleen.

The liver, located on the right side just below the lungs, is the body's major energy factory and part of the body's waste-removal system. It also serves as a blood cell storage area. Sickling blockages can trap stored blood cells in the liver, interfering with its blood cleansing function. In particular, the yellow pigment bilirubin, a by-product of hemoglobin destruction, is normally removed by the liver. But if the liver fails to do this, bilirubin builds up in the blood, and the patient's skin and the whites of the eyes take on a yellowish color. This is called jaundice. Jaundice can also be the result of other problems caused by SCD, which will be described later.

The spleen's blood circulation is served by a system of very small blood vessels and spongelike sinusoids, making it very vulnerable to sickling blockage crises. One of the spleen's jobs is to remove damaged red blood cells, such as sickle cells. It has to work overtime to remove short-lived sickle cells, and it can become clogged with the debris of these cells. The spleen swells with all this added material, and it is unable to perform another of its other major jobs, that of providing the infection fighters needed by the body. As a result the person becomes vulnerable to infection.

The spleen also functions as a blood storage area, storing blood and releasing it when the body needs it. This function may go awry—stored blood is not released when needed. Large numbers of red blood cells are trapped in the spleen. This is called splenic sequestration. In acute sequestration, so many red blood cells may be trapped that the person may die because of lack of blood. This is usually only a problem during the first few years of life for the person with SCD.

OTHER SICKLING DAMAGE

Other organs that can be damaged by sickling blockages are the kidney, the brain, the penis, the eyes, and the ears.

The kidneys have a number of important jobs. They remove wastes from the blood, washing them out of the body in the urine. The kidneys control the body's balance of certain chemicals called electrolytes, which regulate fluid movement within the body. The kidneys also play a role in the production of red blood cells. All of these functions—important to life—can be damaged by sickling blockages. Bedwetting can be a problem for children because the kidney releases too much liquid into the urine.

Sickling blockages depriving parts of the brain of oxygen cause damage to the brain. This is called a stroke. Since the brain is the body's command center, the effects on the person depend on the location of the brain damage.

Blockage in the tiny blood vessels of the penis, the male sex organ, causes a painful stiffening, or erection, called priapism. Sometimes the penis will also swell, and urination will be painful. This painful erection may last from a few hours to weeks.

Sickling blockage to the eyes and ears can produce blindness and hearing loss. Skin ulcers on legs and ankles occur as a result of sickling blockages in skin blood vessels. It may be a year before these sores heal, and they may come back.

ANEMIA: THE SHORT LIFE OF SICKLE CELLS

Sickle red blood cells are also the victims of sickling blockages. The cells may become permanently sickled after a number of sickling events or an extended one. The spleen, liver, and bone marrow destroy old red blood cells and damaged ones, such as permanently sickled cells. In contrast to a normal red blood cell life of 120 days, sickle cells live only 10 to 12 days. The

BLOOD—
A LIFE-NOURISHING LIQUID

Blood is the body's trucking system, water supply, and sewage system. It is a thick liquid containing red blood cells, white blood cells, and much smaller platelets. Red blood cells (erythrocytes) carry oxygen from the lungs to different parts of the body. White blood cells (leukocytes and lymphocytes) fight infection, and platelets initiate clotting when the body is cut.

About 45 percent of blood is blood cells—about 700 red blood cells for every single white blood cell and 20 platelets. The liquid part of the blood contains all the substances the body is transporting: nutrients from the intestines and oxygen from the lungs as well as waste to the kidneys, lungs, and skin. Other substances in the blood include hormones made by glands, substances that maintain the body's pH level of slight alkalinity, proteins that fight infection, and proteins that will take part in clotting should a blood vessel be broken. Blood is a mirror of most of what is going on inside us; a blood test can give a doctor much information about how our bodies are working.

Much of the liquid part of our blood comes from the foods we eat and the liquids we drink. Most food and liquid is processed in different parts of the body and then passed into the blood.

The blood cells are made in the inner part of the bone called the bone marrow. A new baby has bone marrow in all of his or her bones. As the child grows, fatty marrow replaces the marrow in the bones of the legs and arms and in some other bones. By the time the person is an adult, only the flat bones—ribs, sternum (breastbone), vertebrae (backbone), clavicles (shoulder blades), skull, and hip bone—have blood-manufacturing bone marrow. Samples for testing are usually taken from the sternum or the hip bone.

The bone marrow is stimulated to make red blood cells when the oxygen content of the blood supply to the bone marrow is low. Low blood oxygen may be caused by anemia, hemorrhage, red blood cell destruction, poor blood circulation to the marrow, or exposure to high altitudes where oxygen in the air is low.

Most types of white blood cells are made in the bone marrow. Others are made in the spleen and lymph nodes. Infection stimulates the production of white blood cells. The spleen, bone marrow, and particular kinds of liver cells destroy old and deformed red and white blood cells.

Hemorrhage triggers the production of more platelets, which are manufactured as certain large cells made in the bone marrow, spleen, and lungs break up. As blood is shed, the platelets disintegrate, providing proteins that trigger the clotting process.

SCD patient can be in a constant state of anemia (not enough red blood cells) and therefore a lack of hemoglobin to move vital oxygen around the body. Severe anemia can make a person feel tired, out of breath, light-headed, and too weak to move about. The hemoglobin within the destroyed red blood cells is converted to bilirubin. If this builds up in the blood, the person becomes jaundiced.

Normally, the bone marrow moves swiftly to produce new red blood cells as needed. But the SCD patient may have other problems that sabotage this effort. The bone marrow may be damaged by sickling blockages in its sinusoids; or the body may lack the raw materials needed to make red blood cells. Folic acid found in many foods is one such substance. The body of the person with SCD may run low on these chemicals during the body's constant effort to make new red blood cells. Infection may interfere with the formation of new red blood cells or kill the new cells.

Kidney damage from sickling episodes may mean that the kidney cannot play its role in red blood cell manufacture. The damaged kidney may fail to cleanse the blood of wastes that block the action of the bone marrow. Damaged kidneys may make less erythropoietin, a chemical that triggers bone marrow manufacture of red blood cells.

As mentioned earlier, the body's constant destruction of red blood cells produces a great deal of bilirubin, a by-product of the breakdown of hemoglobin. The liver removes this bilirubin from the blood and makes it into bile. Some of the bile is passed into the intestine and some is stored in the gallbladder and passed out later to the intestines. So much may end up in the gallbladder that the bile crystallizes out into small pebbles called gallstones. Gallstones may simply cause indigestion or, in some cases, severe pain if they travel into the bile duct leading to the intestine. If the gallstones block the duct, the bilirubin backs up into the blood, causing jaundice.

OTHER ABNORMAL HEMOGLOBIN GENES

There are other kinds of genes that produce different kinds of hemoglobin that can pair with the HbS gene to cause a different, usually milder, disease.

People with one HbS gene and one HbC gene usually have a milder kind of SCD, with fewer and less damaging sickling episodes. The C hemoglobin separates the sickle hemoglobin crystals, keeping them from sticking to one another.

Another hemoglobin gene is called the beta thalassemia gene. Normal genes make beta protein chains, an important building block of hemoglobin. There are two variants of the beta thalassemia gene: One makes no beta protein, and the other makes very little. The person inheriting a HbS gene and a beta thalassemia gene may have typical symptoms of SCD or a very mild condition, depending on the kind of beta thalassemia variant inherited.

Another kind of hemoglobin can also affect the severity of SCD. This is fetal hemoglobin made by the unborn baby as it grows inside the mother. Some people continue to make fetal hemoglobin after they are born. In some way not really understood, fetal hemoglobin protects those carrying a pair of HbS genes so that they often have only mild symptoms of SCD. Even small babies born with a pair of HbS genes are protected by the fetal hemoglobin still in their systems until they are about six months old.

People inheriting one HbS gene and one normal HbA gene are said to have sickle cell trait. They do not have SCD. They may have a few minor problems with

29

their kidneys and spleen related to sickling events, but in general their health is good.

A GLOBAL PATTERN OF THE SICKLE GENE

The mutation, or change, in the hemoglobin gene that produced the HbS gene took place in the bodies of some people perhaps three or four thousand years ago. For some reason, when the gene split during the formation of a cell a mistake was made. This mutation took place in people living in five different parts of the world: Central West Africa, Atlantic West Africa (Congo, Zaire), Equatorial and Eastern Africa, Central Cameroon, and either Central India or Eastern Saudi Arabia. During normal splitting of cells in the body, the HbS eventually ended up in the person's eggs or sperm and was passed to the children and eventually to the children's children. Usually mutations go unnoticed if they do not harm the person. On the other hand, a mutation that harms the person will disappear because the person usually dies without producing children or cannot produce children. The mutation is not passed on.

In the case of HbS, people inherited only one HbS gene. They did not have SCD. These people lived in the tropics, where malaria is a serious disease. Malarial parasites invade the body's red blood cells, where they multiply. Sickle hemoglobin in the red blood cells is believed to create conditions in the blood harmful to the malarial parasite. A person carrying a natural resistance to malaria is going to have good health and live to produce children. The person without sickle hemoglobin in the blood may not survive. Thus this mutation spread through the population. As people traveled and moved, married and had children, the HbS gene was carried to other areas and thrived where malaria was a problem.

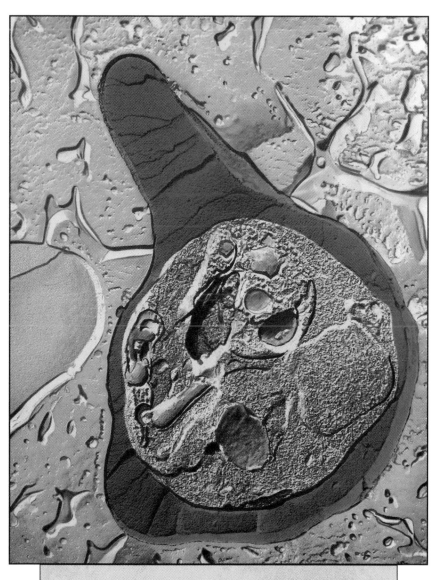

An electron micrograph shows the malarial parasites growing inside this red blood cell.

Today the HbS gene is found in people living in equatorial Africa; the Mediterranean areas of Portugal, Spain, Italy, Albania, Greece, Turkey, Syria, Israel, and North Africa; and in Saudi Arabia and India. In some parts of Africa, 20 percent carry the HbS gene. The figure is the same for the population of some villages in northern Greece, Saudi Arabia, and four Indian states. The gene has been carried—mainly by the slave trade— to the Caribbean, North America, and Northern Europe. In the Caribbean area, the malaria factor takes hold to favor the HbS gene—one out of ten people carries the gene. But in Northern Europe and North America, where malaria is not a problem, the incidence of the HbS gene is much lower and usually only found in black people. About 8 percent of American black people carry the HbS gene.

This process in which a beneficial gene takes hold in a population is called natural selection. But there is a bad side to this particular case of natural selection. As the HbS gene thrived, it became more likely that a man and woman both carrying one HbS gene would marry. A man and a woman who both carry the one HbS gene have a one in four chance of producing a child with two HbS genes. A double dose of the HbS gene is hardly a beneficial effect. This child would have SCD, a far worse problem than malaria.

It is estimated that, worldwide, 250,000 babies are born with SCD each year—100,000 of these babies with SCD are born in Nigeria.

For three centuries—the 1600s through the 1800s— nearly 10 million Africans, many carrying the HbS gene, were shipped to the Americas. Today estimates are that 70,000 black Americans have SCD. Just twenty-five years ago, a person with SCD could expect to live about fourteen years. But today the life expectancy for a person with SCD extends through the late forties. More is known about ways to relieve or prevent some of the SCD complications. Physicians using this knowledge can put their patients on the road to a longer and less painful life.

Chapter Three

CONTROLLING SICKLE CELL DISEASE: LIFESTYLE AND TREATMENT

The camp is located in the woods of Connecticut. Everywhere you look, children are having fun. In the heated swimming pool, a boy in plaid trunks jumps high to catch a basketball. A girl in a pink bikini skims her hand across the water's surface, creating a mighty splash that lands on a boy riding a yellow rubber ring. Nearby, in the woodshop a ten-year-old boy is fastening the wheels onto a toy car he is making for his little brother. Over near the edge of the woods, other children are camping out in a tent. Shouldering their fishing poles, they head down the hiking trail to the lake to try their hand at catching fish. They use save-a-fish hooks and let the fish go after they catch them.

These children all have SCD. The fun they are having at camp fulfills Dr. Lee Pachter's vision of the goal he has for his young patients with SCD. "I want

Dr. Lee Pachter

each child to have a healthy functional life," says Pachter, Medical Director of St. Francis Hospital and Medical Center Sickle Cell Service in Hartford, Connecticut.

Some twenty years ago there was no way to help those with SCD. But in 1986 researchers discovered that daily doses of penicillin could prevent serious infection and in turn a great deal of the severe pain and tissue destruction caused by SCD. It was found to be important that babies with SCD begin taking penicillin soon after they are born. Testing all newborn babies for SCD is now routine in most of the United States.

Pachter begins seeing babies with SCD right after birth. "We see SCD patients as a multidisciplinary team—a physician, nurse educator, nutritionist, and social worker," says Pachter. The team helps the patient and family deal with and prevent the physical as well as related emotional and social problems of SCD.

THE NEW BABY WITH SCD

Pachter sees the newborn child every two months. The baby is not likely to feel the effects of SCD for six months, but Pachter needs to spend time educating the parents about SCD and how to be good caregivers.

Pachter realizes that parents may be devastated by the news that their child has a disease that may cause severe pain and stroke, and that the child will have to endure the disease as long as he or she lives. "It has to be a terrible shock," he says. "I tell the parents that none of the bad things they've heard about may happen to their child. A lot has changed in caring for children with SCD. Symptoms are variable; some children don't get very sick."

Pachter tells the parents, "You have a beautiful, healthy, perfect baby. I expect that to continue." He tells them to treat their child as a normal child with just a few precautions.

"The key to treatment of SCD is to get the parents—and later the patient—to see themselves as the primary caregivers," says Pachter. "I give them advice and walk them through certain situations. But they give the care. I give the guidance and they learn to take control of the disease." The parents know they can always call Pachter in an emergency.

He gives them a small folder—a pain passport, which is kept updated about the child's health problems and pain medication needs—a kind of mini-medical chart. This they can give to any other doctor providing emergency medical care.

THE DOCTOR'S INSTRUCTIONS

After examining the baby and ordering blood tests and a chest X ray, Pachter describes to the parents how sickled cells block the blood vessels and cause pain and damage to the body. But he explains that there are ways to prevent this from happening some of the time. Then he describes the preventive approach, the key to which is preventing infection. He writes a prescription for penicillin and tells the parents to give this medicine to the child every day. During the first year, in addition to giving the usual baby shots, Pachter immunizes the baby against flu and hepatitis B, providing more protection against infection.

The child will need a high-calorie, high-protein diet, because those with SCD use more energy. Since sickle cells only live about two weeks compared with the four-month life of normal red blood cells, the child needs lots of nourishment as well as daily doses of folic acid for making new red blood cells.

The child must be given lots of fluids to thin the blood so that it flows faster. The fluids also keep the sickle hemoglobin molecules from touching each other and forming crystals. If a child gets overheated, the body perspires and loses fluid. Getting too cold will

37

make the blood vessels constrict, making it more difficult for sickle cells to move through smaller vessels.

Pachter trains the parents to check the spleen, just below the ribs on the left, for swelling. They should do this every day. The parents learn how to deal with the child's pain—a heating pad or warm towel on the place that hurts, pain medicine, water or juice, and rest.

After a few sessions with Dr. Pachter, parents know how to care for their child. Each time they return, he reminds them about the penicillin, folic acid, fluids, and other things he's taught them.

THE TODDLER WITH SCD

Pachter sees toddlers every three months. This is the time when swelling of the hands and feet, severe infections, and splenic sequestration (trapping of most of the blood by the spleen) usually occur. Pachter checks the child for signs of these conditions and reminds the parents to be on the alert. He immunizes the two-year-old against pneumococcus, a bacteria that can cause pneumonia and septicemia (blood poisoning). The child also gets annual flu shots and is immunized against meningitis, an infection of the covering of the spinal column and the brain.

Pachter begins involving the child in caregiving when he or she is about two years old. "You have to tell your mom or dad when you hurt and where you hurt," he says, "Say 'Mommy hurt' and show her where it hurts." Pachter knows that quite often children with SCD link hurting to hospitals and needles. "I try to make them understand that it's important for their mother or father to know when they have pain."

Children four years and older visit Pachter twice a year. Now there is concern that pain crises may have harmed vital organs. The heart and eyes are checked, and blood tests are done to check kidney and liver function. Since diseased teeth are an infection focus, the child is scheduled for dental exams twice a year.

THE OLDER CHILD LEARNS TO TAKE CHARGE

As the children reach school age, Pachter begins to bring them into the discussions about their care. They need to remember to get lots of fluids—milk, water, juice, popsicles, and gelatin fill the bill. If they have pain or it is a very hot day, they should drink even more. When they are playing sports or taking gym, they should take time out when they feel tired and drink more fluids. They should remember to take their penicillin and folic acid and to eat a healthy school lunch of meat, vegetables, potatoes, milk, and fruit.

By the time the child becomes a teen, he or she knows the routine of preventive care. Pachter knows that there are special problems for teens with SCD. He checks the hip joints for damage by sickling blockages. He checks the gallbladder and asks the patient about pain, nausea, and vomiting, symptoms of gallstone disorders. Boys may be concerned about priapism (painful erections). Pachter advises them to take a warm bath, drink lots of fluids, and take pain medicine. "If that doesn't help, call me," Pachter tells the patient. If he gets a call, Pachter usually puts the patient in the hospital where he uses special medicines and treatment to relieve this painful and troubling problem.

TEENS WITH SCD

Teens learn about sexuality and the proper kind of birth control to use if they have SCD. Some kinds of birth-control pills can bring on sickling blockages. Girls are warned that pregnancy may bring on severe SCD symptoms. They are urged to think about the chance of having a child with SCD. The message is that there are only two ways to prevent pregnancy: either don't have sex or use birth control.

Leg ulcers related to sickling blockages usually occur during the teen years and into adulthood. For some reason, the problem is more common in males. The ulcer usually begins as a small raised crusty sore just above the ankle. The doctor examines it and checks to make sure the ulcer isn't caused by some other condition, such as varicose veins or diabetes. Then the patient is advised to clean and disinfect the ulcer, wear special stockings and shoes, rest, and keep the leg elevated. If this does not work, other surgical procedures performed in the hospital can be used to heal the ulcer.

Teens with SCD tend to be smaller than other teens and they develop sexually a few years late. They may ask when they will be like other kids. Pachter says, "Don't worry. It's going to happen—later—but it's going to happen." But they want to do what some other kids do and may be tempted to drink alcohol or smoke. Dr. Pachter warns them that alcohol causes the body to drain off fluid and that dehydration can bring on a sickling crisis. Also, smoking can sometimes cause a chest sickling crisis.

HOSPITAL CARE

Sometimes, despite the preventive lifestyle program, serious problems occur. Pachter is always there to deal with emergencies. He trains the parents and the patients to have a watchful eye for signs of an emergency. In addition to a swollen spleen and severe pain, parents must watch for a fever of 101 degrees; yellowing of the whites of the eyes; pale gums or fingernails; swelling of hands, feet, or abdomen; chest pain or breathing problems; paralysis; and weakness. These signs usually signal a sickling crisis, and the patient is hospitalized.

In the hospital, Pachter treats severe bone pain and priapism pain with intravenous fluids, heating pads, rest in a dark room, and strong painkillers, such as morphine. Pachter knows that the pain is bad and so he gives large doses of morphine at first, then gradually lessens the dose. There is a concern that giving the patient morphine will produce addiction. "Patients, and even some doctors, worry about addiction. We have some teens who are in a lot of pain but don't want any morphine because they fear addiction," says Pachter. But he is fortunate to be able to consult with a doctor at St. Francis who is a leading authority on the use of drugs to kill pain. "You will never addict a patient if you control the pain. Partial pain control—or none at all—causes the patient to seek more and this leads to addiction," says Pachter.

Chest syndrome affects the body's oxygen supply and is very serious. Patients afflicted with rapid breathing and chest pain have a number of things going on all at once: sickling blockages of the blood vessels, perhaps infection, and oxygen starvation. Pachter gives them fluids to ease the sickling and blood transfusions to provide them with normal blood cells that can do the job of carrying oxygen and won't sickle and cause more problems. They get morphine for the pain, antibiotics to fight the infection, and oxygen. Sometimes the battle will be lost, and the child will die.

CARE FOR STROKES

During mid- to late-childhood, strokes caused by sickling blockages in the brain are the problem to watch out for. Depending on the part of the body it affects, a stroke can impair learning and thought, vision, speech, and use of muscles. Severe headache, seizures, or weakness may be signs of a stroke. When a parent calls Pachter with this report, he hospitalizes the patient. Once it is confirmed that the patient has had a stroke, he begins treatment.

A patient who has had one stroke will probably have another. And that stroke could be fatal. Pachter gives the patient a blood transfusion. A transfusion can prevent a second stroke because it provides nonsickled red blood cells that dilute the sickle cells so that they will not clog the blood vessels that serve the brain. Also it fools the body into not making more sickle cells. Patients who have had a stroke will get blood transfusions every four to six weeks.

In mid-1998, researchers reported on a test using sound waves (Doppler) that can detect conditions that precede a stroke. Using this test would mean that transfusions would only have to be given when prestroke conditions are detected.

TREATING SPLENIC SEQUESTRATION

Another serious condition that Pachter treats with blood transfusion is splenic sequestration—a dangerous condition in which the spleen traps most of the body's blood. The child arrives at the hospital weak and pale and with a swollen abdomen due to an enlarged spleen. Pachter gives the child blood transfusions to provide the body with badly needed blood. The child is given intravenous fluids, pain medicine, and antibiotics to make up for the infection-fighting spleen that is now out of order. These patients will also get transfusions every four to six weeks to forestall a future problem.

"We usually remove the spleen when the child is about two years old if the child has repeated problems with sequestration," says Pachter. Most children who don't have severe problems with sequestration experience so much splenic scarring from sickling blockages that by the time they are about five years old, thespleen has shriveled up and disappeared.

Aplastic crisis also brings the patient to the hospital. A parvovirus infection stops the body's manufacture of red blood cells and the patient is very anemic. Transfusions restore blood to the system, and after about a week the bone marrow recovers and starts making red blood cells. This is a one-time emergency because the person's body develops an immunity to the virus.

Leg ulcers that do not heal with home treatment are treated in the hospital. A special bandage soaked in zinc oxide, called an Unna's Boot, is applied to the ankle and shin area. If this does not help, the patient is given transfusions to supply the skin area with normal oxygen-carrying red blood cells that won't cause sickling blockages. Surgical repairs with skin grafts or the transplant of large pieces of tissue from other parts of the body are a last resort for ulcers that haven't healed after more than six months.

WHEN PATIENTS ARE AFRAID AND SAD

Hospitalization is very stressful for children who feel abandoned by family and isolated in the midst of severe pain. Even at home, they cannot do things they enjoy and the things their friends do. They may suffer anxiety, depression, fear of death, and low self-esteem. Pachter and his team provide help for the emotional and social problems the young patients and their families may have to deal with. In particular, it is important to relieve the emotional stress, since this is one factor that is thought to bring on sickling blockages.

All team members do psychiatric counseling, and the child may be referred to a developmental psychologist who specializes in chronic illness. But when a child brings up an issue, Pachter responds. When a child asks, "Am I going to die?" Pachter gives a straight answer. The child may have seen friends with SCD die, and knows it's possible. Pachter says, "You have an illness and because of that illness you have a higher risk. I can't say 100 percent that you're not going to get very sick. I can't say 100 percent that you're not going to die. But we can and you can do things to decrease that likelihood." Pachter doesn't downplay the child's concern. Rather, he suggests that he or she talk to a psychiatrist or perhaps a religious leader.

When it comes to self-esteem, Pachter believes that nothing builds one's self-worth better than achievement in sports and other activities. He realizes that parents think of their children as vulnerable and don't encourage them to take part in sports. But he doesn't want his patients living in a glass bubble. It's true, children with SCD have to take breaks to rest and drink fluids, but they can do sports.

LOOK! I'M DANCING!

Pachter, through the use of a grant, has arranged for classes in dance and karate for two dozen of his patients. The instructors gear the classes to the special needs of the children, and Pachter is there to keep an eye on everybody.

Peek into the dance studio, and you see three- and four-year-olds in leotards or T-shirts practicing for their June recital. "Up to the ceiling, down to the floor . . . right and left and pow, wow, pow," they chant.

Next door, the room is dark as the karate class for older children warms up. Eyes closed, with a tape

This three-year-old gets help putting on her tap shoes for a dance class she looks forward to.

playing the sound of surf, the children meditate. "I am . . . I am . . . I am strong. I am healthy . . . I love myself." Once they have warmed up, they practice their karate kicks and moves.

Pachter believes the sessions are helping. And parents agree. One mother of a four-year-old described her daughter as shy and noncommunicative. But now the girl is opening up a lot more. "She came out of her shell. She knows the songs and she loves coming here."

The meditations for the older children also help them deal with the everyday aches and pains of SCD. Says one eleven-year-old, "If I feel sick, I kiss myself and look in the mirror and say 'I love myself' and I'll meditate a few minutes." It seems to help. Based on this discovery, Pachter is now trying to set up Yoga and Tai Chi programs for the children.

Other programs and activities for young people with SCD have been arranged by the Connecticut chapter of the Sickle Cell Disease Association of America. There is a summer program at a camp for ill children that has a fully equipped infirmary staffed with doctors and nurses. A six-week, half-day "Fun on the Farm" summer program gives children the chance to ride horses, learn how to care for farm animals, and do other chores such as grooming the horses. The farm experience is a challenge that builds confidence and strengthens self-esteem, says the program director. Coming up in the future is a summer work program at St. Francis, during which young people can earn money.

THE SOCIAL WORKER: THE PROBLEM SOLVER

Nancy Caperino is the social worker on Pachter's team. Each time the patient and family see Pachter, they also see Caperino. She talks to them to find out if there are problems. If there are difficulties with giving the care the patient needs, she may suggest that a nurse visit to help them with strategies for remembering the medicine or making sure the child gets fluids and nourishing foods.

She asks if there is extended family or some other support system that can help the parents. If not, and if the family feels overwhelmed by child care or dealing with behavioral problems, Caperino may suggest a parent aide. These volunteers visit once or twice a week and serve as special friends who listen, give encouragement, and help solve problems.

Is the child having problems in school? These can be caused by frequent absences due to illness or perhaps brain damage caused by strokes. Perhaps testing will determine the child's weaknesses and strengths. Then strategies are developed to help the child to learn. Caperino will go to the school with the parents and perhaps talk to the teachers about special help the child might need. She will alert the teacher to the child's need for fluids and the consequent need for frequent bathroom breaks. She will talk to the school nurse about the child's condition and give the nurse medicines that the child might require.

If the problems are financial, Caperino will steer the family to low-rent housing agencies; to utility programs that will maintain service during winter for a small monthly payment; to Social Security, which will provide some monthly income to a child with severe illness whose family income is low. If someone in the family needs work, she will direct them to vocational training programs.

For some parents, emotions interfere with their ability to care for the child. They may feel guilty because the child got the condition from them. They may be angry, hostile, or depressed. Perhaps they need

ELECTROPHORESIS: THE DETECTION OF DIFFERENT KINDS OF HEMOGLOBIN IN THE BLOOD

Electrophoresis uses the fact that different kinds of hemoglobin will migrate in different ways when exposed to an electrical current.

The blood specimen is first treated to separate the red blood cells from other cells and substances in the blood. Then a chemical is used to remove the hemoglobin from the cells.

A small amount of the hemoglobin solution is then placed on a flat, thin square of gelatin. The gel square is placed in a frame, and the frame is inserted in a container of liquid called a buffer. A buffer controls pH—it is important to keep pH constant during the procedure.

An electric current of fifty volts is passed through the specimen on the gel square for thirty minutes. The square is dried and stained. The different kinds of hemoglobin show up as blue blots on the square.

Solutions (standards) known to contain the kinds of hemoglobin being tested for are also placed on the gel square. The technician compares the pattern of movement of the standard and the specimen to determine the kinds of hemoglobin in the specimen.

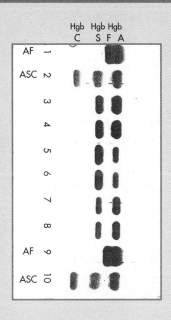

In this copy of a stained gel square, the standards are at the top and bottom in positions 1, 2, 9, and 10. Patient specimens are in the middle positions, 3 to 8. Migration is from the positive pole to the negative pole, right to left. Right to left you see hemoglobin A, then fetal hemoglobin just ahead, seeming to be joined to hemoglobin A. Next is sickle hemoglobin. The results show that all patients have hemoglobin A and sickle hemoglobin. They have sickle cell trait. A specimen showing nothing in the A line and a large blob in the sickle line would have SCD. The standard has hemoglobin C, but no patient has C.

49

to seek psychiatric help, or a support group where they can share feelings with other parents.

If the child needs counseling, Caperino does some of this or may send the child to a psychologist.

St. Francis Sickle Cell Service sponsors events that bring a lot of what Pachter's team does into one place for families of those with SCD. The service sponsors weekends at camp where entire families can share outdoor activities and camp experiences. Workshops will deal with some of the problems they all live with. This event is a kind of culmination of the team's mission to meet the medical as well as the social and mental-health needs of the entire family of a young person with SCD.

ADULTS WITH SCD: ON THEIR OWN

Pediatricians and hematologists watch over all aspects of the care of their young patients with SCD. But the day comes when a patient becomes an adult and leaves the care of a pediatrician.

As Bridgeport, Connecticut, nursing administrator Claudia Edwards says, "It's easy to love and comfort a child with SCD . . . but adults with SCD often need as much." For many adults with SCD, the issue is relief of pain. Says Edwards, speaking to a group of health professionals, "When they say they have pain, believe them." Many medical professionals are not aware of the excruciating pain SCD can cause and do not understand the pain medication needs of those enduring sickling pain. Just a few minutes of talking to a patient in pain can clear up the misunderstanding.

Take, for example, a patient that hospital nurses labeled hostile, disruptive, and a clockwatcher seeking drugs. "He was loud, abusive, and demanded his painkiller before it was due," one nurse wrote on his chart.

Thirty-six-year-old Gil (not his real name) had suffered many of the classic problems of SCD during his lifetime: destruction of part of the bones of one shoulder, leg ulcers, pneumonia, and priapism. Now he was in the hospital suffering from excruciating pain in his left shoulder, arms, lower back, and legs—bone gnawing pain just about everywhere. Gil's doctor had ordered pain medication every two hours. When the two hours ended, the pain came right back. But a half hour passed before the nurse brought his pain medication—for Gil, thirty minutes of suffering and complaining loudly that he needed his medicine. Not until Gil left the hospital was it discovered that the nurse had given the medication at a certain time and recorded it half an hour later when she returned from her medication rounds to all her other patients. Thus Gil's chart showed that his medication was due half an hour after he was supposed to have it.

A similar problem occurred for a thirty-four-year-old man with SCD who was labeled hostile and a drug seeker by an emergency room staff. During psychological counseling it was discovered that the medication he was given to take at home was insufficient to stop his pain. He was denied a refill at the pharmacy because his prescription read "no refills," and so he turned up in pain at the emergency room once or twice a week, loudly demanding medicine for his pain. He was given a prescription that adequately dealt with his pain, and his frequent visits to the emergency room stopped.

Many adults with SCD have learned how to stand up for themselves and get through the bad times.

Twenty-five-year-old Hertz Nazaire describes his pain as feeling like "being stabbed many times with a knife . . . like firecrackers going off in my bones." Having SCD and being sick all the time make him depressed. But he has joined a support group and finds that sharing his problems with others who have SCD helps. Sometimes Nazaire meditates: "I think of a nice place like the beach and that helps the pain." Nazaire is a talented artist who finds that painting helps the pain. Some of his paintings hang on the walls of New York City's Montefiore Hospital.

Nazaire now takes a new medicine for SCD called Hydrea, and his pain is better. "You gotta be strong when you have sickle cell," he says.

Forty-year-old Tom Harper complains that most people think he's about twenty. He remembers being in constant pain as a child, missing weeks of school. In 1985 he nearly died from an infection. He's had painful ulcers on his heels. One hip has been replaced because of infection and he now uses a walker to get around. "Now I don't get sick a lot. I've learned how to take care of myself, not to push myself," he says. He works as a volunteer for the Sickle Cell Disease Association. "I tell people about SCD. We have to work together to get rid of it. It would be good to find a cure," Harper says.

Kenita Dickerson is a thirty-two-year-old college graduate who works as a guidance counselor helping troubled children. She remembers the pain and strength of her mother who also has SCD. Dickerson remembers a painful crisis when she was twenty-five years old. She was hospitalized with excruciating pain. Then just recently she was hospitalized with double pneumonia and a very high temperature. Now Dickerson has learned what she has to do to take care of herself. She eats right, she gets fluids, exercise, and rest. "I meditate, I relax, I keep a balance in my life," she says. She's learned what seasons of the year are bad for SCD. She's tried herbs for pain and swears by a well-known painkilling ointment. "I try to learn everything I can about SCD. If I see something new about SCD in the paper, I look up more information on it," says Dickerson. She is about to move to another city for a new job. And her first move will be to "network with those who know about SCD."

Chapter Four

DISCOVERING THE WHY AND HOW OF SICKLING

For all of his life, an American slave had suffered the pains and sickness of the Chweecheechwe disease, as some called it back in his native Africa. One day in 1846, the desperate man ran away from his master. But he killed another runaway slave during an argument, and that was the end of his short run for freedom. He was caught, tried, found guilty of murder, and hanged. A doctor who autopsied the slave's body was astonished to discover that the slave had no spleen. The autopsy report included other details that described the organ and bone destruction you read about in Chapter Two. The doctor didn't realize it, but he had described what we know today as sickle cell disease (SCD). That autopsy report is the first written description of SCD. The slave had lost his spleen to the sickling blockages of SCD.

SIGHTING SICKLE CELLS UNDER THE MICROSCOPE

In 1904, Dr. Ernest Irons, an intern at Chicago's Presbyterian Hospital, got the first look at the cause of SCD. Looking through a microscope at the blood of a young college student, Irons saw sickled red blood cells. He drew the curved, slender, banana-shaped cells on the blood report form so that all could see what he had seen through the microscope.

The patient, twenty-year-old Walter Noel, had come from Grenada, West Indies, to Chicago to study dentistry. The blood laboratory report showed that Noel was anemic and that he probably had an infection. Although he had to take time out from his studies for hospital care for his illness, Noel graduated with his class and returned to Grenada. There he practiced dentistry until he died of pneumonia at the age of thirty-two.

By 1922, several more cases of the blood disease were discovered. From Dr. Iron's drawings of the sickled red blood cells came the name for the condition—sickle cell anemia, changed in the past few years to sickle cell disease.

THE ROLE OF OXYGEN IN SICKLING

In 1927 a simple observation by an Indianapolis doctor, E. Vernon Hahn, provided the first information about why sickling takes place. While studying a patient's red blood cells under the microscope, Hahn noticed that the sickled cells in the blood sample were all in the bottom of the test tube. When he shook the tube, the sickling went away. Hahn knew that shaking had mixed oxygen into the blood. Could oxygen play a role in causing red blood cells to sickle?

Hahn put together an apparatus to test this idea. He fitted a glass slide with a chamber in the middle with a small gas inlet. The patient's blood was placed in the chamber, and the slide was placed under the microscope lens. Hahn watched the red blood cells through the lens as different gases were allowed to flow through the chamber. The cells sickled when oxygen was very low.

Hahn wondered if it was the red blood cells or their hemoglobin content that reacted to low oxygen. He removed the hemoglobin from the cells and observed the cells in a low-oxygen environment. The empty cells did not sickle, and so Hahn knew that hemoglobin caused the sickling.

Once sickling had been traced to hemoglobin, scientists turned their attention to studying this complex protein. In 1940, Irving Sherman, a medical student at Johns Hopkins in Baltimore, found that sickled cells and nonsickled cells transmitted light differently. Reading the report of this research, Harvard Professor of Medicine Dr. William Castle realized that there was some change in the hemoglobin molecules within the sickled cells.

During a meeting with other physicians and California Institute of Technology (Caltech) chemist Linus Pauling, Castle mentioned this finding. Castle, who had recently lost a patient to SCD, described some of his work. Studying the blood vessels of an Italian American woman with SCD, Castle discovered the cause of her pain and sickness to be the slowing or the blocking of the blood flow by sickled red blood cells. He had seen what he called deformed or sickled red blood cells clumped together in her blood vessels.

SCD: THE FIRST GENETIC DISEASE DISCOVERED

Pauling had done some work on hemoglobin, and Castle's information gave him an idea. Biologist George Wall Beadle, Pauling's colleague at Caltech, was studying the ways in which mutated genes could cause

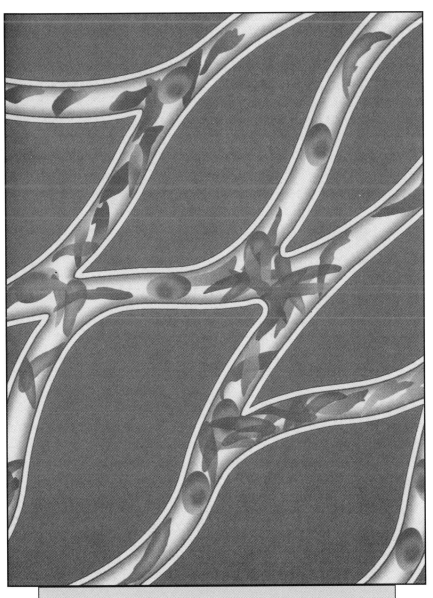

The long, banana-shaped sickle cells do not flow easily through blood vessels, creating blockages.

disease by directing the manufacture of defective protein molecules. Pauling wondered whether SCD might be a molecular disease. Could a mutated gene have produced an abnormal hemoglobin molecule?

Pauling gathered a team of researchers headed by Dr. Harvey Itano and asked them to find out whether blood from SCD patients contained abnormal hemoglobin. The team turned to a new chemical technique called electrophoresis, which separates proteins. They tested blood from healthy people and from people with SCD. Indeed the blood from people with SCD contained a different kind of hemoglobin molecule.

Since the hemoglobin molecule was made according to the chemical blueprint of a gene, people with SCD had a pair of mutated genes different from the normal. In a 1948 paper entitled "Sickle Cell Anemia: A Molecular Disease," Pauling wrote that it was "a clear case of a change produced by a [mutated] gene." SCD was the first molecular disease discovered.

Thinking about this new discovery, and applying his knowledge of chemistry, Pauling theorized that these abnormal molecules might have sites on their surfaces that would attract them to one another. A kind of crystalline clump would be formed, deforming the red blood cell into sickled shapes.

Studies by John Harris in 1950 proved Pauling's theory. Harris found that sickle hemoglobin deprived of oxygen becomes very thick. Microscopic views of the sickle hemoglobin showed parallel alignment of hemoglobin molecules into elongated crystal-like masses resembling sickle cells.

GENETIC FLAW FOUND

In 1956, Vernon Ingram found the flaw in the hemoglobin molecule. Using a protein called an enzyme,

Ingram broke normal and sickle hemoglobin into segments. Using electrophoresis, he compared the segments, finally narrowing down to one sickle hemoglobin segment that was different from the comparable segment in normal hemoglobin. Breaking down that abnormal piece, Ingram located the single amino acid that was different: He found valine where glutamic acid should have been.

In the early 1960s, British scientist Max Perutz found the reason why the sickle hemoglobin molecules stick together and form crystals. The location of the mutation—where valine had replaced glutamic acid—was on the surface of the huge, coiled hemoglobin molecule. Valine has an electrical charge that draws the sickle hemoglobin molecule into the outer surface of another sickle hemoglobin molecule.

Meanwhile in the African country of Northern Rhodesia (now Zimbabwe), British researcher E. A. Beet found the connection between resistance to malaria and sickle hemoglobin. He noted that blood from people with sickle cell trait—one HbS gene and one normal gene—contained less malarial parasites than blood from people with two normal hemoglobin genes. Another physician working in Zaire found that people with sickle cell trait seldom were afflicted with malaria.

Other studies showed that sickle hemoglobin protected against malaria, particularly in children. Children's immune systems are not yet developed well enough to protect them from malaria. Thus, children especially benefited from the malaria resistance of sickle hemoglobin.

RELIEVING THE SYMPTOMS

Meanwhile in the 1950s and 1960s, Howard University researcher Dr. Angela Ferguson focused on relieving the

Dr. Angela Ferguson

pain and sickness of SCD. She was a pediatrician who
had begun her research by studying the growth and
development of black babies. But her work soon
brought her to the bedside of babies with SCD. She
knew this was an inherited disease, but little was
known about genes, and thus a cure would be slow to
come. And so Ferguson focused on the symptoms of
SCD and ways to relieve them.

Ferguson and her team sorted through the symptoms and found that they varied depending on the age of the child. From birth to two years, children suffered pain and swelling in the ankles and wrists. From two to six years, pain and swelling of the abdomen was the most common symptom, caused by problems with the liver and spleen. From six to twelve years, symptoms were mild, flaring up thereafter. For teens, skin ulcers on the ankles were a common problem.

But then a sad case of a six-year-old boy who had his tonsils removed taught Ferguson that there might be no typical symptoms for those suffering from SCD. The anesthesia given to the boy before the surgery brought on a stroke. The boy was unconscious and paralyzed for several days. He recovered slowly. But he had four more strokes and died a year and a half later. An autopsy showed a brain badly damaged by strokes caused by sickling blockages. The boy had shown no signs of SCD for all of his six years. From this case Ferguson learned that those with SCD must be given large amounts of oxygen after surgery to prevent strokes.

THE ROLE OF INFECTION

Ferguson wondered what other circumstances besides anesthesia might bring on a sickling crisis. She kept a day-by-day account of the health events, small and large, in the child's life. Then, when the child had a sickling crisis, Ferguson would check the health diary. Quite often infection came before a crisis. Blood tests done during a crisis showed that the blood was thicker and not as alkaline as it should be.

From this information, Ferguson developed a plan of treatment for preventing crises. First of all, the treatment would be in the home and carried out by the parents. She advised parents to encourage the child to drink lots of water. This would thin the blood. The parents were told to keep a bottle of water in the refrigerator especially for the child, and tell him or her to drink the bottle empty. Parents were told to add a small amount of bicarbonate to the water to make the blood less acid.

An infection prevention program was developed. Colds were treated early on. Parents were told to keep their children away from sources of infection, such as sick people. Ferguson advised nutritious food and vitamins to build resistance. Good dental care would prevent infected teeth. The treatment philosophy that was developed by Ferguson remains in use today.

Ferguson also dealt with the notion that children with SCD were retarded. She realized that their appearance made them look retarded. Some had a slight point to their heads and they were small, due to the effect of SCD on bone growth. But testing showed most children with SCD had normal IQs. Ferguson traced most troubles with schoolwork to absences due to illness.

In the 1970s, researchers at Yale University studying infections in children found that the rate of infection for those with SCD was about the same as that for children who had had their spleens removed. It seemed that SCD might damage the spleen. The doctors believed that dealing with infection might help patients with SCD. They decided to run SCD tests on all children coming to Yale New Haven Hospital for care. Those children found to have SCD were enrolled in a special clinic. The Yale SCD testing program and clinic were the first in the United States.

The clues about infection found at Howard and Yale were studied at the National Heart, Lung, and Blood Institute (NHLBI). In 1986, NHLBI researchers found that daily doses of penicillin reduced the rate of pneumonia among children with SCD. Since then, children with SCD are given penicillin from birth throughout their childhood. This practice seems to keep them infection-free.

Research that followed has focused on how infection brings on sickling and ways to prevent sickling or cure the disease.

BETTER MEDICINES AND CURES ON THE HORIZON

Finding new medicines for an illness begins at the lab bench where an idea is tested. Then it may be tested in animals and finally in people with the disease who volunteer to take the new medicine and be tested for good and bad effects. If the medicine works in the volunteers and causes no serious side effects, it can then be approved and doctors may write prescriptions for it.

Bob (not his real name) was changing the oil in a car when he felt a dull ache in his ankles. When the pain began traveling up his legs, Bob knew another sickling crisis had begun. Soon he was in terrible pain and on the way to the hospital. He knew he was in for another three weeks of pain. But a doctor made an offer of an experimental treatment, and Bob couldn't refuse. He signed his name to an agreement to be a test subject for a proposed new medicine. The new medicine was injected into his blood. Four days later, he felt much better.

A Maryland financial analyst we'll call Richard was making twenty trips a year to the hospital for treatment of sickle cell crises. Then he agreed to take some new experimental pills every day. His frequent trips to the hospital ended.

Bob and Richard were participating in the testing of two of a number of new medicines being developed for the treatment of SCD. These new drugs are directed at the factors that bring on sickling crises. Much research has uncovered these factors.

A PROBLEM OF STICKINESS

Research done in the 1980s and 1990s has provided an understanding of the processes within the blood vessels that might lead up to a sickling crisis. An important clue was found in the blood of patients with SCD. Endothelial cells shed from the inner lining of the blood vessels were found to be activated; that is, proteins produced in response to infection, injury, or irritation had made the cells sticky. This response is called the inflammatory response.

When these activated endothelial cells and sickle cells were mixed together in a test tube, they stuck together. The walls of damaged, permanently sickled cells were found to have areas that will bind to the sticky endothelial cells lining the blood vessels. So when injury, infection, or irritation makes the cells lining the blood vessel sticky, the person is vulnerable to a sickling blockage.

These study results led to a more detailed theory of why a sickling blockage occurs. After all, people with SCD have circulating sickle cells all the time, but they don't have sickling blockages all the time. When a permanently sickled cell sticks to an endothelial cell made sticky by inflammation, other cells pile up behind it. The roadblock produces an oxygen-poor environment. Unable to move on to oxygen-rich areas, the trapped cells begin to sickle. It is a vicious circle. The blockage maintains the low oxygen content. More and more cells pile up and sickle. More studies will have to be done to prove this theory.

But given the evidence doctors already have that infection and temperature often precede sickling crises, the sticky theory seems quite likely. Research projects are under way to discover if drugs that fight inflammation—such as steroids and nonsteroidal anti-inflammatory drugs (NSAIDs), such as ibuprofen and naproxen—can prevent or relieve sickling crises. It was such a research project that Bob volunteered for.

Fifty-six children in several Dallas hospitals also volunteered to test the effects of steroids on pain episodes. The children received two injections of large amounts of steroids for two days in a row. Their severe pain crisis was cut short. These results indicate that reducing inflammation can break down sickling blockages. But steroids can have dangerous side effects, such as high blood pressure and tissue destruction. The children in Dallas suffered no bad effects. But steroid treatment of SCD needs more study to determine safe dosages and long-term effects.

Another medicine, RheothRx, a kind of lubricant, which inhibits the sticking together of endothelial cells and sickle cells, is being tested and may soon be used to relieve severe pain crises.

FETAL HEMOGLOBIN: MADE BY THE UNBORN

Observations of blood from different kinds of people have led to another approach to treating SCD. These observations involve fetal hemoglobin—hemoglobin made by unborn babies. After birth, the baby's bone marrow stops making fetal hemoglobin and switches over to making hemoglobin A, adult hemoglobin. In the case of the child born with SCD, that adult hemoglobin is hemoglobin-S. But that new baby with SCD still has a great deal of circulating leftover fetal hemoglobin, which lasts for about six months. In 1948, Dr. Janet Watson theorized that fetal hemoglobin protected babies with SCD, and this is why they don't have problems with SCD until they are about six months old. People with SCD who live in Saudi Arabia and certain Indian states continue to make fetal hemoglobin after birth. Most have very mild SCD.

If fetal hemoglobin protects against SCD, perhaps a good strategy might be to find a way to restart the body's fetal hemoglobin factory. It's in the bone marrow, right where sickle hemoglobin is made.

Hydroxyurea, a drug used to treat cancer, has been found effective in stimulating fetal hemoglobin production, and it is relatively safe. It was approved for treating adults by the FDA in 1998 and is also being used to treat children. Hydrea, as it is called, was the medicine taken by Richard, whom you read about at the beginning of this chapter.

Not only does Hydrea stimulate the fetal hemoglobin machinery, but it also produces other effects that relieve sickling. These effects are prevention of inflammation and dehydration of HbS, both believed to trigger sickling.

Now many doctors are prescribing Hydrea for their SCD patients. Dr. Sue McIntosh, a Connecticut pediatrician, calls it "lifechanging" for the children she treats. She notes that seventeen of her patients taking Hydrea for an average of three years now have a total of eighteen pain crises a year compared with ninety-

GETTING NEW DRUGS APPROVED

The Food and Drug Administration (FDA) regulates testing and approval of new drugs. Testing of a drug must be done on animals and then humans to determine its effectiveness and safety.

Drugs are tested on animals to learn how they are taken into the body, carried throughout the body, broken down by certain organs, and eliminated by the body. The way the drug works in the body, and its safety, are also determined. Of particular concern is whether the drug may harm babies that may be conceived. Many drugs fail this preliminary testing because they don't work or because they are too harmful.

Drugs that are successful at the stage of animal testing are issued an Investigational New Drug (IND) Application by the FDA. This means that the drug can now be tested on humans.

First the drug must be tested on healthy human volunteers, then on volunteers who have the disease the drug is meant to help. Researchers test to find out if the drug helped the sick person and if it caused any bad reactions. The relationship to the volunteer's age, sex, other diseases, and other drugs the patient might take must be studied. All of this information from animal and human studies must be submitted in the form of what is called a New Drug Application (NDA) to the FDA.

The FDA studies the NDA and after two to three years may approve the new drug. Even after the drug is made available to sick people, the manufacturing company, doctors, and pharmacists must be on the alert for side effects. If serious side effects are found, the FDA may withdraw its approval.

three per year before they started. Their day-to-day sickling aches and pains have also decreased. McIntosh also noted improvement of asthma and allergies in her patients, which may be an indication of Hydrea's anti-inflammatory effect. But the new drug does not seem to prevent other problems caused by sickling blockages, such as bone and spleen destruction.

Studies are under way to determine if combining Hydrea and erythropoietin might produce greater quantities of fetal hemoglobin. Erythropoietin is a chemical made by the body that stimulates the manufacture of red blood cells.

NITRIC OXIDE: A NEW IDEA

It has long been known that low oxygen content in the blood of people with SCD brings on sickling of the red blood cells. In 1977 researchers discovered that nitric oxide gas makes the hemoglobin molecule change shape. But it was not known what effect this shape change had on the qualities of hemoglobin itself. Could it improve the ability of HbS to hold onto oxygen?

In 1997, Harvard researchers wondered if this discovery could be used to design a treatment for SCD. They recruited nine people with SCD who were not in a sickling crisis at the time. After the volunteers had inhaled the nitric oxide gas for forty-five minutes, tests were done on their blood. Eight volunteers proved to have blood with an improved ability to combine with oxygen. The researchers wondered if the gas would cause sickled cells to unsickle, thus relieving a crisis. They have begun a project with sixty volunteers to test their ideas. If the results are good, more testing will follow to confirm the results. Tests on volunteers will also determine whether inhaling the gas causes any bad side effects. The next step is to present the experimental data to the Food and Drug Administration (FDA) for approval. If the treatment receives FDA approval, the gas could be supplied in an inhaler. Daily inhaling of nitric oxide could prevent or relieve the sickling of red blood cells.

Nitric oxide is the active agent in nitroglycerine given to patients with heart trouble because it dilates the heart's blood vessels, and thus provides more blood to the heart. Researchers have found that nitric oxide dilates blood vessels in the lungs and proved that it helps new babies with lung problems breathe better. Nitric oxide is now approved for use in newborn babies in respiratory failure.

The question now being studied is whether nitric oxide will help SCD patients with chest syndrome crisis. Inhaling nitric oxide eased the breathing of one child dying of SCD chest syndrome. Within three days, the child was off the respirator, breathing on his own, and soon went home. Twelve other children suffering from chest syndrome were also successfully treated with nitric oxide. More study will be done to make sure that nitric oxide inhalation is a safe and effective treatment for chest syndrome and other SCD crises.

WATER LOSS FROM THE RED BLOOD CELL

As you know, dehydrated sickle hemoglobin forms the troublesome crystals implicated in sickling. Water loss through the cell membrane causes the dehydration. But why does the cell lose water? It has to do with the slight acidity of the blood of those with SCD, something discovered by Howard University's Dr. Ferguson in the 1960s. Scientists now know that electrolyte ions potassium and chloride carry water out of the blood cell. Is there a way to stop this water loss? Reducing the acidity of the blood might be the answer. Studies on mice and on patients with SCD showed that alkaline magnesium supplements reduced the acidity of the blood; water loss from the red blood cell was reduced by 50 percent. Dehydration of sickle hemoglobin was reduced and, in turn, sickling was, too.

The red blood cell can also lose potassium and water when calcium ions enter the cell. A drug used to fight fungus infections—clotrimazole—was tested on sickle cells and found to stop loss of water from red blood cells. Blood counts done on patients with SCD who took the drug also showed that fewer cells were becoming permanently sickled and destroyed. The red blood cells of the patients were healthier and living longer.

Doctors and scientists believe that combinations of the drugs you have read about might be the pills of the future for those with SCD.

BONE MARROW TRANSPLANT: RETOOLING THE BLOOD CELL FACTORY

While pills made from some of the substances mentioned above should help the person with SCD, that person will always have red blood cells containing sickle hemoglobin. But a procedure called bone marrow transplant, which has been tested since 1991, cures SCD. After a transplant, the person's bone marrow no longer makes red blood cells containing sickle hemoglobin.

The tests were carried out on seventy patients in hospitals in the United States and Europe. A major concern in any transplant procedure is the immune response. The body normally attacks any protein foreign to it, such as disease organisms or allergens, that enters. When the body attacks transplanted cells, it is called graft rejection. For this reason, patients about to have a transplant are given drugs that prevent an immune response. As you may expect, these drugs make the person vulnerable to infection, so strong antibiotics are also given. In the case of a bone marrow transplant, strong drugs are given to kill the patient's own bone marrow.

The cells from the donor can also have an immune response in the patient, in effect attacking the patient's cells. This usually fatal condition is called graft versus donor host disease. Because of this, the blood and tissue proteins of the donor and patient must be matched. Generally a patient's brother, sister, or parent have the best chance of matching.

Once the patient has been prepared with the different drugs, the bone marrow transplant procedure is done. The bone marrow is removed from the donor's hip bone while the donor is under anesthesia. It is then injected into the patient's vein. The marrow stem cells—those that make red blood cells—migrate to the patient's bone marrow cavities and begin to multiply. The patient's bone marrow is replaced, and the new marrow begins making red blood cells that contain normal hemoglobin.

Of the seventy patients with SCD who received bone marrow transplants between 1991 and 1995, fifty-three were declared cured, after a two-year followup. Of those who were not cured, seven died of SCD-related problems or donor host disease. Some had graft rejection and had to continue on treatment for SCD.

In these studies a cure rate of about 75 percent was achieved. But the researchers believe that selection of candidates could improve this rate. They believe that bone marrow transplants aren't for everyone with SCD. The patients should be young and should not have suf-

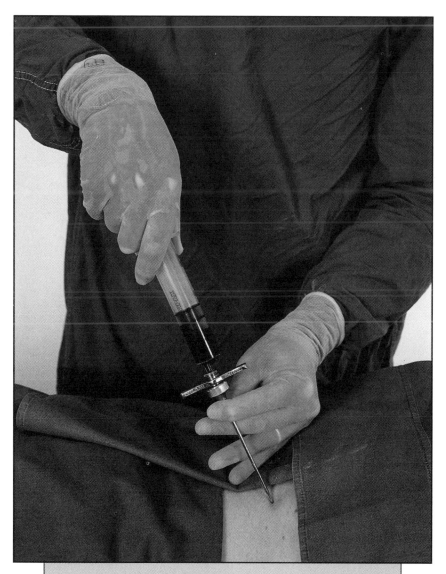

A bone marrow transplant in progress. Marrow is suctioned through large needles placed in the bone at the top and back of the pelvis.

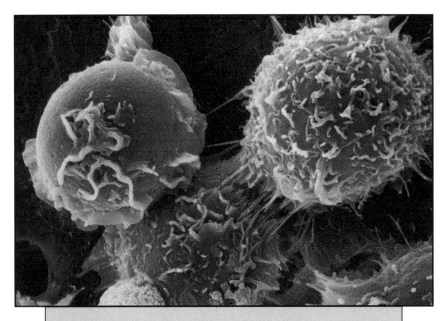

Umbilical cord stem cells

fered any serious effects from SCD, such as lung or kidney disease. The researchers think that blood transfusions, which introduce a number of foreign proteins into the body, may sensitize the immune response system and cause graft rejection. For this reason they believe that patients who have had a long series of transfusions should not have bone marrow transplants.

Researchers had another idea that might produce better bone marrow transplant results. Why not use the blood from the umbilical cords of new babies, something that is usually discarded after the cord is cut. This cord blood is rich in stem cells, is less likely to contain disease organisms, and most important, is more likely to be a match for the patient's blood since a new baby has not yet developed the large quantities of proteins that cause rejection. In one study, cord blood transplants were done on 562 patients suffering from various blood diseases, including SCD. Eighty-five percent had successful transplants.

GENE TRANSPLANT

Another possible cure being studied is gene transplant—transplanting a normal gene into the cells of a person with SCD. The carrier is a virus. Viruses are cell invaders that move into the body's cells and take over the cell's machinery. That is how they make us sick.

One amazing discovery that makes gene transplant possible is that of proteins that can split genes away from chromosomes and other proteins that can splice viruses onto genes. The normal gene is removed from the chromosome and spliced to a harmless virus. Then the gene/virus splice is mixed with cells from the patient's bone marrow. The virus carries the normal gene into the marrow cells. The marrow is injected back into the patient's marrow. But in tests of this procedure to date, the treated cells produced very little normal hemoglobin.

Duke University scientists have tried an innovative approach to gene transplant. The gene is the command center for making hemoglobin. It sends out a messenger chemical (messenger RNA) carrying the chemical blueprint for making the hemoglobin. Why not change the messenger's instructions? It works in a test tube, but of course the real test is to see if it works in people, where all kinds of other things besides hemoglobin manufacture are also going on.

Chapter Six

PASSING ON THE GENE

Entertainer Tionne "T-Boz" Watkins of the TLC music group has SCD. She is the National Celebrity Spokesperson for the Sickle Cell Disease Association of America. She tells people about the pain of SCD she has known. It is inherited, she says, and urges people to "do the proper thing, get tested, and make informed decisions about parenthood." She tells them that at least 70,000 Americans have the disease. T-Boz raises questions: Could you have the gene? Could it be in you? If so, can you possibly have babies that don't have SCD? Where can you get tested?

It is these kinds of questions that bring couples to genetic counselors. Calling on new knowledge about genes, SCD, and new techniques, the genetic counselor tells the couple about all the possibilities. "I'll tell you about the risks and the tests and procedures," the coun-

T-Boz, a singer in the popular music group TLC

selor says, "but you must make the major decisions about what you want to do."

LEARNING ABOUT SCD

The counselor explains the inheritance of SCD. The couple learn about sickle hemoglobin, how it distorts the red blood cells, which block blood vessels, in turn causing pain and damage to the body. The couple are urged to talk about the possibility of having a child with SCD. How would they handle it?

If the couple want to know whether they carry the hemoglobin S gene, they are sent to a genetic laboratory facility to be tested. The couple then meet with the genetic counselor to discuss the results. If neither of them or only one of them has the hemoglobin S gene, there is no possibility that any child they have will be born with SCD. But if both have a gene for hemoglobin S, there is a 25 percent possibility that they will have a child with SCD.

Then the counselor tells them more about SCD. She tells them about the strokes, terrible pain, and severe lung disease SCD can cause. SCD kills some children. But SCD is a variable disease, and some people have few problems. More and more is being learned about the disease, and this knowledge is being used to ease pain and treat other problems.

MAKING A DECISION

"So you have to decide whether you want to take the chance of having a child with SCD. If not, don't have children. Adopt," says the counselor. "But if you do decide to conceive a child, there are ways to know before it is born whether the baby has SCD. Then you could choose to have a fetus with SCD aborted." The counselor then describes two techniques that can be used to test the fetus.

One technique is called chorionic villus sampling (CVS). Chorionic villi grow out like tiny fingers from the outer membrane surrounding the growing embryo and attach to the wall of the uterus to form the mother-child attachment called the placenta. Using an instrument called an ultrasound scanner, the doctor can see the baby and the placenta. He or she then inserts a needle into the mother's abdomen or a tiny tube into her uterus and removes a few chorionic villus cells from the placenta. In the laboratory, a chemical is used to make the cells multiply. Then a technique using fluorescent dyes tests for defects in the gene. CVS is done between the tenth and twelfth weeks of pregnancy and is believed to be very accurate. But there is a slight risk that the test may cause defects of the hands, feet, tongue, or jaw—or even death—to the fetus.

Another test can be done during the twelfth and eighteenth weeks of pregnancy. Using a technique called amniocentesis, a syringe is used to remove some of the fluid from within the inner membrane surrounding the fetus. The fetus's skin cells in the fluid are tested for the hemoglobin S gene.

If the testing shows that the fetus has SCD, then the couple must decide whether to have the child or have an abortion. Once more, the counselor tells them that SCD is a variable disease that may cause many problems or very few. They are reminded that much can be done to ease the pain and treat the problems and that more treatments are being studied.

The couple may feel they cannot allow their living fetus to be killed. Or they may feel that allowing a baby to be born with SCD is a cruelty to that child. Some couples decide to keep their baby. Those who do not are referred by their doctors to abortion services clinics such as Planned Parenthood, Inc. In the clinics, the couple meet with a counselor who asks if they have thought carefully about their decision to abort their fetus. "Do you really want an abortion?" they are asked. If they still want the abortion, the fetus is surgically removed from the mother's uterus through the vagina. An abortion is best done by the twelfth week of pregnancy because abortion beyond that time is a risk to the mother.

FERTILIZATION IN THE LABORATORY

A couple may ask, "Can we avoid CVS and deciding about abortion? Is there any way to make sure a baby we have doesn't have SCD?" "There is a way," says the counselor, who then describes a technique called *in vitro* fertilization. Eggs from the woman and sperm from the man are placed in a laboratory dish. There the eggs are fertilized by the sperm. The fertilized egg begins to divide into more cells. Within five days it has divided into sixteen cells. At this point one cell from each fertilized egg is removed and tested for the two hemoglobin S genes that cause SCD. An embryo without SCD is implanted in the woman's uterus. The embryo develops into a fetus and is born as a child without SCD.

In vitro fertilization is available at many locations in the United States, including the Faulkner Hospital in Boston. Most health insurance plans will pay for the procedure.

THE WOMAN WITH SCD

Females with SCD also meet with counselors. For them, the question is "Can I have a baby?" The counselor's answer is "You can, but it's risky to you and the baby." There are many things a woman with SCD must understand about the kind of stress pregnancy puts on her body, which can harm her and, in turn, the child. Pregnancy can worsen her disease, bringing on problems such as acute chest syndrome, seizures, congestive heart failure, severe pain episodes, severe anemia, and urinary tract infections. Kidney disease; high blood pressure; alcohol, tobacco, or drug use; or taking a great deal of medicine for pain are other factors that can complicate pregnancy.

Sickling blockages may affect the tiny blood vessels of the placenta, the mother-child connection attached to the uterus. This plate-shaped structure passes oxygen and food to the baby from the mother and removes wastes from the baby's body, passing them into the mother's body. Sickling blockages can interfere with this vital transport system, harming the baby.

There can be complications when the baby is born that result in the death of the baby. The baby may be very small or born with defects caused by lack of oxygen. And the mother must face the possibility that her child will be born with SCD. How will she care for a child with SCD when she herself is dealing with a sickling crisis?

A woman who fears the risk and does not wish to get pregnant is told that there are only two ways to avoid pregnancy: either don't have sexual intercourse, or use contraception (birth control). The woman can also elect to be sterilized, which takes away her ability to conceive and bear a child.

PREGNANCY AND SCD

If a woman with SCD does become pregnant, she is put into a high-risk pregnancy care program. The first task is learning about the physical effects of her SCD that may cause complications during pregnancy. Such effects may include liver and kidney disease caused by sickling blockages, anemia, and increased amounts of iron in the body. Anemia (low blood hemoglobin) is the result of continuous red blood cell destruction endured by those with SCD. Excess iron is a leftover from the continuous destruction of red blood cells and hemoglobin, which contains iron. Should any of these problems be discovered, measures are taken to deal with the complications they may cause during pregnancy.

The woman must visit her doctor at least twice a month. She may have to be hospitalized or be ordered to bed during the pregnancy. During labor and delivery, every care is taken to avoid distress to the mother and baby. Anesthesia and blood transfusions may be given to the mother. Oxygen and intravenous fluids are used to avoid sickling crises.

Some mothers with SCD lose their babies (miscarry) before the baby is ready to be born. A few mothers with SCD die during pregnancy. But with good treatment and care, 99 percent of SCD mothers who carry their babies to full term have normal births.

Medical science has brought us a long way from the days when those with SCD didn't live long enough to be parents.

CONCLUSION

First identified in 1904 by a hospital intern, sickle cell disease became, more than forty years later, the first disease found to be a genetic disease. But genetic diseases do not easily yield their secrets—secrets that might help to find a cure.

During most of the past century, countless medical researchers, building on the discoveries of those who came before, have finally tracked the genetic flaw and determined how it directs the formation of abnormal hemoglobin. We now know how this abnormal hemoglobin makes red blood cells sickle and why these sickled cells block blood vessels and cause so much pain and illness. Most of the secrets of SCD are known now.

But more than a hundred years after the identification of SCD, doctors find themselves merely at the threshold of treatments and cures for this painful and destructive disease. Painstakingly working through every step of the process that causes red blood cells to sickle and block blood vessels, researchers have tried to find medicines that would stop one of those steps. Now doctors have at their disposal a new medicine called hydroxyurea, which seems to take aim at several of those steps. And their patients are helped—less sickling, less pain.

Can the flawed gene that makes sickle hemoglobin be changed? So far, there isn't much hope of that.

Is there a cure? Ask thirteen-year-old Keone Penn. Young Keone had endured just about everything SCD could do to a person: terrible pain, infection, fever, even temporary stroke. Twice-a-month transfusions held his SCD at bay. Then his doctor suggested a bone marrow transplant with blood cells from the umbilical cord of a newborn baby. Keone would get a new blood-making system that would make normal blood cells. It was experimental, might not work, and could be fatal, said the doctor. Figuring he might die anyway, Keone agreed to the transplant. It was tough going for a while after the transplant; Keone suffered fever, diarrhea, and liver and intestinal inflammation. But one year after the transplant, Keone's bone marrow was making normal red blood cells that didn't sickle. His doctor called him cured. And Keone is looking forward to living the life of a normal boy.

That's a happy ending for this story of terrible pain brought on by a flawed gene.

Dr. Andrew Yeager and Keone Penn
celebrate Keone's sickle-free blood.

GLOSSARY

anemia: a condition caused by abnormally low amounts of red blood cells and/or hemoglobin in the blood. Symptoms include tiredness, paleness of skin and gums, and breathlessness.

antibiotic: a substance made by microorganisms, such as molds, that kill bacteria

appendicitis: an infection of a small pouch that extends out of the large intestine near its connection to the small intestine, located near the right groin

blood count: a measure of the different cells and hemoglobin in the blood

congestive heart failure: a condition caused by the heart's decreased ability to pump blood to the different parts of the body, which results in accumulation of fluid in legs, chest, and abdominal cavity

electrolytes: substances, including ions of sodium, potassium, calcium, and magnesium, that are dissolved in fluid inside cells, outside cells, and within the blood. Electrolytes regulate the movement of fluid from these areas.

embryo: the developing fertilized egg; in humans, the developing organism from one week to eight weeks

endothelial cells: a kind of skin cell that forms the lining of the body cavities, the heart chambers, and the blood vessels

erythropoietin: a complex protein made by the body that stimulates the manufacture of red blood cells

fetus: an unborn developing human after it is eight weeks old

folic acid: a chemical containing nitrogen found in leafy green vegetables and beans that is needed by the body to make red blood cells; vitamin M, also vitamin Bc

fungus: an organism that can vary in size from microscopic (yeast) to large (mushroom)

hemoglobin: a large molecule that coils in on itself to form the shape of a cube. Its role is to transport oxygen throughout the body.

hormones: chemicals produced by glands that direct activities in different parts of the body, such as use of food and kidney function. Insulin, testosterone, and estrogen are examples of hormones.

immunization: the injection of dead or weakened disease organisms to stimulate the body to make proteins that will fight these organisms and thus prevent infection

inflammation: the body's defense system against infection and injury; includes fever and increased production of blood and other fluids

in vitro: denoting biological procedures done in laboratory dishes, compared to *in vivo* procedures done in living creatures.

ion: an atom or molecular fragment that has an electrical charge. Ions react readily with other chemicals.

lymph nodes: small glands, part of a system of vessels called the lymphatic system, that carry fluid that transports oxygen, nutrients, and substances from the blood to the tissues

malaria: a tropical disease caused by a tiny parasite that invades the blood

minerals: substances found in the earth's surface. Some minerals—such as iron, magnesium, sodium, and potassium—are essential to the functioning of our bodies.

miscarry: to expel a fetus from the uterus before the fifth month of human pregnancy

penicillin: an antibiotic made by a mold

pH: a measure of acidity and alkalinity. Measured in units from 1 to 14, with 1 most acid, 7 neutral, and 14 most alkaline.

seizure: a response to an irritation of the brain that produces abnormal electrical discharges, causing such reactions as twitching, chewing movements, numbness, and hallucinations

septicemia (blood poisoning): the invasion of the blood by bacteria

sinusoid: a small channel or chamber for the passage of blood in organ tissue

steroid: a type of fatty chemical that includes hormones and bile

syndrome: a set of symptoms that occur together

RESOURCES

Books

Bloom, Miriam. *Understanding Sickle Cell Disease.* Jackson: University Press of Mississippi, 1995.

Brown, Fern. *Hereditary Diseases.* New York: Franklin Watts, 1987.

Harris, Jacqueline L. *Hereditary Diseases.* Brookfield, CT: The Millbrook Press, 1993.

Lyon, Jeff, and Peter Gorner. *Altered Fates: Gene Therapy and the Retooling of Human Life.* New York: W.W. Norton, 1995.

Milunsky, Aubrey. *Choices Not Chances: An Essential Guide to Your Heredity and Health.* Boston: Little, Brown, 1977.

Thompson, Larry. *Correcting the Code: Inventing the Cure for the Human Body.* New York: Simon and Schuster, 1994.

Wingerson, Lois. *Mapping Our Genes: The Genome Project and the Future of Medicine.* New York: Dutton, 1990.

Zallen, Doris Teichler. *Does It Run in the Family? A Consumer's Guide to DNA Testing for Genetic Disorders.* New Brunswick, NJ: Rutgers University Press, 1997.

WEB SITES
Sickle Cell Anemia
http://radlinux1.usuf1.usuhs.mil/rad/home/case

Sickle Cell Information Center
http://www.emory.edu/PEDS/SICKLE

Joint Center for Sickle Cell and Thalassemia
http://cancer.mgh.harvard.edu/medOnc/sickle.htm

Comprehensive Sickle Centers
http://www.fpg.unc/sickle/index.htm

Sickle Cell Society
http://www.sicklecellsociety.org/

MOVIE
A movie entitled *Warm December,* in which Sidney Poitier plays a doctor, tells the story of a beautiful young African diplomat who has sickle cell disease.

INDEX